This Will Be the Day

Julie Yeager

ISBN: 0692678409
ISBN-13: 978-0692678404 Backwards Hat Publishing

DEDICATION

This book is dedicated to my mother who worked timelessly to create a caring, safe and inclusive environment in which I flourished. By being my advocate with the schools, starting a downs syndrome group for me and my friends, and so many other things, she has supported and encouraged my pursuit of my dream to be a poet and a publisher.

ACKNOWLEDGMENTS

I am deeply grateful to my family for their constant support and unwavering encouragement throughout my life.

This work would not have been possible without the support of Alchemia, Lorin Kaufman and Liz Jahren who believe in me and want to help me make my dreams come true. Without the persistence of Liz this book would still be solely in my imagination. My friends and fellow writers at Alchemia have been my cheerleaders, and an ongoing source of feedback and unflagging reinforcement.

Lastly, I want to thank Mary Lester, my writing teacher at Alchemia, for her guidance and patience. She made me laugh and focus.

Thank you, all.

Julie Yeager
Petaluma, CA
July 2016

CONENTS

THIS WILL BE THE DAY

This will be the day
when ice will melt.
When will the day joy come?

Well start ideas inspiration
can show true facts like
what is he or she wearing?

Trouble has overcome
unbearable under powers wake.

Granted wishes pour water
that drips upon heads
oh sweet lord
we come in peace.

Combine unities closure
must be unattainable
look farther define
how the day has past.

Night began but
emptiness still remains
useless now despair
destiny's hard work.

CELEBRATE

Celebrate holy through
ones self imaginary friend
who can tell me thy name?

Despite humanity
discover unique disposition
hold bond tightly
let go with
only one reason.

Find others who can
treat insanity
honest relationship
that honored gratefulness.

This may change
but just leap
unity has caught forth ahead.

This that back when
tell side shows unified
strength before action
that crashes and burns.

Ending has put after
every story but poetry
never has to stop.
Inspiration is my creative soul.

MAN DAYS

Man days like these
inspiration hits nothing
like jelly on toast.

Find what is useless
others justify learning experiences
but here I am.

Life never without
Meaning comes close
writing will never
loose my ability.

This creative life
my own no one
less can be mistaken.

Heights fail
completes this tale
hide fears.
If only these wet tears
will shed.

My loneliness becomes
vivid will imaginary
become real because
this is how I feel.

GOOD MORNING TIME

Good morning time
days begin and
nighttime well
must need to end.

Special moments open
doors and eye.
Sun is shining so
time to wake.

Rhyme lets wait till
tea, coffee and crumpets.
Imagine England on a
nice happy warm timeless
morning jog.

Hello how are you?
Fine day to sing well
carry on despite my
evening affair.

Morning came again
birds chirping and chirping
must be right time to write.

Creative juices flow but
I'm still here
enjoying a glass of wine
ending my long days.

WILL THIS BE?

Will this be well?
Let me see myself on the
other side of the mirror.

Notice looking across
wondering is this how
I look from behind.

Loud sound of breaking
glass someone must
have tampered with
mimicking my evil Twin.

Wow can't believe
I can only be broken
so quickly.

After one hour I came
to the conclusion that
I have been framed.
Better luck next time.

Remember mirrors can
only reflect how others see us.
I should not have been less
than who I can be
more like myself in other ways.

CHANGES

Changes how lost
my different ways
thoughts stay inside
until pen hits the paper.

Then willingly
can't stop
inspired action just flows
into beautiful poetry
like a caterpillar turns
into a butterfly.

Ask me anything but
never call me late for dinner.

Showing encouragement is
what I came here for
faith will bring a smile.

Changes sensed
comfort shall this pay
must be mine to say.

Shame has nothing to say
I surely need myself to stay
changes may delay.

TIME

Time for sleep
not for me
excite my inspiration.

Lights may be off
but my brain is still in shock.

Can't sleep
people talking
inside my head
telling me to not
put down the pen.

Why must my big head
filled with bricks
inspire my poetic features?

I want to be famous rich
and still keep my humor
while I laugh into the night.

Even though I am bored
I keep writing.
Why is that?

Can someone explain to me
why I drank that last cup of coffee?

Join hands gather
send on emotions carry
but love keeps undone.

STARS

Stars go to sleep why cant I?
Question I would like to know.

While dark night sky lasts so do I
that's the reason why.

My poetry is now
exciting to be writing.

Sleep not on my mind
late yes I am aware.

It is 1:00 In the morning
and I have to get up
about 8:45 so I can
catch the van for the
Alchemia day program.

Then well I should get some rest
but I can't sleep
I can only write.

Well determination has its rewards
no wonder I feel I am in a rut.

I need to move on and move away
to do all the things I want to do
like being famous to do all the
things in New York.
Well who knows?

INSPIRATION

Inspiration never sleeps.
Why? Well, don't ask me.

I need a doctor maybe not
I need a rest yes
I want one indeed.

But how can I sleep with
inspiration keeping me awake?
Can I breath now?
It's getting late and
I am not tired. Only thing
I keep doing is writing.

Someone hear me
please let me out
I want some sleep
I am too much for my youth.

Wow my poetic soul
never shuts up.
Darn damn I am
not only awake but
now I am writing
an epic novel.

My laughs over joys
hidden treats but
my whole world is my poetry
as you well know.

I CAN'T

I can't and I won't
over think my power or
dreams not yet clear
I need balance.

When Alchemia starts
that's when I run to success
American novel will write
epic yes well
knowledge serves me Justice.

Stand up for Special Needs
stand up for people with disabilities
here I am
this is who I am.

Let me be the judge, president
or even no one with a label
me Julie another same one
to talk to and for listening
as well.

Never labels can be put
on you without me knowing
no one at all without knowing
no one at all you can always
lean on me forever.

BELIEVE

Believe in me
I am here.
No one will pass as a nothing
because we are something
to love.

My Alchemia my family
is devoted to you
always yes
we can do this.

Stand up for what
needs to be.
Alchemia has power and love.
I will stand up and
be a leader.

You can follow me on my
journey to success and fun
hopefully I will get my career
as a famous and rich poet.

Alchemia is helping
me to self publish. In the
Alchemia day program
we have fun classes
and teachers who
believe in us.

THIS IS MY HOME

This is my home Santa Rosa
Alchemia my home away
from home.

I escape to my world
let me be
if I want to do art
that's who I am inside.

Sometimes when
I leave Alchemia
I feel lost. It seems
like I lost a friend
when really I am empty inside.
Why is it that way?
Well let me tell you.

Nobody knows me but myself
and when I write my poetry
I am complete.
When others show concern
about my health
I want to hide.

This is me.
I don't know how
to say this to them.
I just want to be alone.
If I eat the wrong thing
I will pay the price.

But please stop
with telling me
what I can or cannot eat.

That is my choice
not anyone else's.
Let me make my own choice
I am an adult.

Some people won't eat
a certain way let me
be.

I will do so if
I need help I will ask.

I may have flaws
but who doesn't.

If I mess up like I used to
I always want to be treated
the same as my siblings
whether I have Down Syndrome or not.

I have been keeping this
inside a long time.

But don't get me wrong
I love everyone around me.
When I am treated nicely
then I won't feel this way anymore.

I understand concerns
but when they are about me
I think I am the bad guy
I realize about other people
what they want for their own child.

But when adult life kicks in
that means I want to move on
so let me.

It is hard to see someone fall
but let them see
in their own eyes.

I am not only young but strong
with feelings so delicate.

What is my next
big thing? I know
older siblings get
married or have a baby.

But when it is my turn
to want something and do it
I am sick and tired of
people saying "don't eat that
that's bad for you" or
"You look like you have double chins"
or even after buzzed haircuts.

I just want to be me
so please let me
I want to feel like
I belong.

SELF-POEM

Julie Yeager, is she a big time poet?
Not yet half way but on the road to success.

Julie Yeager, is she in a rut?
Well I'm not sure
living behind my mom is
where I am now.

Julie Yeager, two older siblings
Emily and William
yes I do have them.
Also mom and dad
yes I know I have.

Julie Yeager goes to Alchemia
on her way to her future
yes she is.

Julie Yeager has love and more but
I, Julie am in search of
more and more.

Julie Yeager someday
on top of the world
poetry and creative writing
her own world it still is.

Julie Yeager, author
how does that sound?
                    Boy she can write.

DESPERATE

Desperate well maybe a little bit
but faith, love, rainbows and stars
will keep Inspiration alive.

Nothing will change
for me writing is all me
everything to me
strict writer oh yes I am.

But always has a
smile for everybody
I say hello world.

I have risen to
all there is in my
inspirational views.

Power is mine.
Let me create my destiny.

Show me what I want to see.
How I can be the somebody
I want to be.

Entire night finally came to a close
when rain was silenced.

No noise filled room
dreamless as I lay
nor thy slumber calmly drifted
through thin air.

SUDDENLY

Suddenly rain just falls
pours like cats and dogs
so hard no
person is seen.

No man or woman
taken for granted
by each other and
rain still pours.

Drop after drop
water must come down
then turn into flat puddle.

Earth interesting
how world functions
delight such eco friendly
environments to live in.

Glory has sent but
this will be left to
carry on.

Together forever in days
we have here and now
start what's worth it.

Maybe nothing at all
seems unrealistic from
thoughts and concerns that
are unaware of this timelessness.

OPEN YOUR EYES

Open your eyes
where is that ground
coming out from nowhere.

Hiding well my friend
who could have
been here last.

Anyone knows the answer
judging blank faces tells us
nothing considering darkness
where no man was found.

Listen no voices were in earshot
but footsteps came near
only one was there
with wild imagery.

Noises never found why
how foolish this seems
open all these doors
but stay far.

No danger became of this
sometimes people confuse thoughts
as one's true soul mate.

Believe willingly others
who realize life from
realistic views towards forgiveness.

FRIENDS

Friends should always
take sides even when
they need this mostly
friends make each other
respect them.

Discover when every
minute of everyday
was noticed before
winter started no one
had much on mind.

Consider that dysfunctional
mental fear plays with
emotionally damaged
dark sided past
but leave behind.

Breaking down never fixes
solutions find self
then remain useful
that's going to be the day.

Imagine friends staying
connected even when
times are tough but
I should be taking
my own advice but
eventually I will soon.

NEED YOU

Need you here with
me now that I can
be free going back
just while I am
thinking.

Why should we
part when I am
stuck on you
please never
hold back.

There is only less
than second chances
despite one's own
original plan.

Redemption never
the last expectations
will disappear when
reason seems unattainable.

Grasp opportunities before
they fly away
assume unexpectedly
enough came without
explanation.

Information kept creation connected
in touch with inner energy.

HARD

Hard to say but
nothings seem easy
better off speechless.

Temptation flawless
needs resentment
should maintain absence.

Destroy emptiness within
follow own path
encourage positive direction.

Close let no person criticize
another's own way now
they live maybe what they do.

Decide
let selfish pride
get treated just the same.

Why people judge
well that's not relevant
to their own perspective
opinions.

LET

Let me be me
before these temporary
unlisted items
randomly take charge.

Mostly indescribable
issues can make changes
not as surely possible
but please take care.

Nevertheless may all types
fill empty buckets
take one for the team but
I still am waiting.

Let experience shine
let no one take away
keep it stronger
than one's self.

Let opportunities fly
style has nothing
let self-pity seek elsewhere.

Till tomorrow let's be free
hair willy nilly as described
jumbled in a bunch.

Long like lion's mane
I have no control
until summer when
I go buzz buzz.

LIFE

Life never without
happiness fades today
changes just turn me away.

Friends come and go
family stands by you
but why do they want to
take happiness away.

Extremely challenging
trying to be happy.

Then feels like crap
the next trying hardest
to put all in words.

How can I move on
with light at the
end of the tunnel
burned out?

Well now you know
'cause I have happiness
one day but later
it's been taken away.

PULL

Pull away
hide under blankets
I don't need pity
crap that's all I get.

Family sometimes can
be stuck on one thing
and leave behind the rest.

Well that's how it is
apparently I have one thing
I only care about and that's
 what I am doing.

As we speak
writing is my escape
but sensitivity is all
that has come in my direction
hopefully I can feel better soon.

Want to be left alone?
But all I hear is stupid stuff
that makes no sense.

PROBLEM

Problem is eating food
makes me happy but
others judge on how
I look to them.

Ugly as I feel the more guilt
has fire burning me inside.
Can I be happy?

Being the youngest
in my family blows
'cause anything I say or
do for myself is always
wrong in their eyes.

I get reminded everyday
that I have gained weight
and that's not healthy.
              Why is that?

CONSTANTLY

Constantly being bullied
by people who love me
who are concerned about me
and won't leave me alone.

Why don't I get a brake?
Am I worth nothing?
But this is not in my head.

Nobody sees it my way
everyone has to see it in two ways.
When can they just focus
on me and only me?

What I see complicates
when fingers are pointed
while emptiness drowns
my given pride.

I follow a path somehow
somewhere a curve gets
the better of me.

WHY

No idea why that is but
when rain pours then I
shall melt with deep emotion.

Crazy as that sounds
inside my head seems real
my own opinion.

Never acknowledge why
this has some to be ignored
but why shall we answer
why every time?

Not anything done
loneliness seemed disappointing
why is that so?

If only why was ever enough
said no women not another woman
will breathe such a word.

Are we home yet?
Why must we stop?
Let's loose all whys forever again.

So we made this ride home
quickly as possible without
breathing another why.

To hear nothing but silence
a spin for the last hour
never thought why again.

DAY IN A LIFE

Best day here
where day in a life starts
near beautiful purple flowers
makes days sweet.

Growing when full bloom stands tall
what a sight to see.

When life has never stood
before us we surely give
more thoughts to the table.

Day in a life remains
realities truth seeks
they will find.

Secrets may then hear clearly
another day should be here
when you least expect it.

Redemption caused rain to pour
boohoo planet earth spins towards
this day in a life today.

STRING WORDS

Follow my words carefully
inspiration got the better of me.

Confidence strings words
to fit this puzzle where
could they in this poem
I have written.

Feedback all the same
but love making people
smile while reading these poems.

I stand up in pride for
people who have special needs.

Showing happiness is
how I create my lasting life
my future.

Love me for me
inspire all of those who want
positive friendships.

Here I am not
stringing my words
but the world cares
and so do I.

MAKES ME CRY

Why has pain brought tears?
Look in a mirror.
Who is looking back?

Makes me cry even when
happiness stirred me right
but never state too many
wrongs.

Come join hugs with less beers
'cause that's never the answer.

Besides what's more important?
Taking for granted
never became graceful.
Pick and choose your own battles.

Shortly soon must
take water from eyes
seriously makes me stress free.

Watch clock
remember my shoulder
make that lean when you need.

Don't bother to cry
I will be there for you
every time.

WAITING

Mail never came
box so empty still waiting
next day came but
nothing was sent.

Odd it has been
over a month
still no sign
waiting time is
of the essence.

Manage this waiting thing
boredom as I write the
waiting poem.

Sure this should be complete
but today must leave
me speechless.

Dude waiting
for inspiration to hit
maybe I should
fade to grey.

Waiting for ending of poem
but why wait until
I write again?
Yay my wait is over.

VERSION OF ME – I

Welcome here we talk
only about what's next
never let the past drag
down deep inside
let versions collide.

Depression left when door closed
now let's focus on reality
versions of me happening now
we turn another page.

Same mistakes I have doubted
but maybe survival can reach
towards timeless struggles and
choices.

Published ambitions found
complex concerns cracked
grins never meant to break.

Emotions imagine inner thoughts
make critical mental disrespectful
mess.

What the hay
this consumes matter
ok the point never got made
but what the hay.

Explain how these consumptions
played a part with those who implied
what the hay once more.

Early attraction tossed aside words
that were not the same
so consider these as repeated.

What the hay
tired of miscommunication
powers that melted.
Well please don't ask just consume
all that's been heard before.

Can you only imagine?
A question I can't seem to answer.
Certainly never do I take
my own advice.

Life matters.
But when some person talks
does anyone fill in the blanks?

Damage has been done
but by no affection
advice beheld by another
cry visions collide.

Fiction has nothing to do with
what's been written here
my words want
what matters most heartfelt.

No one understands true meaning
when words are just so
hard to pry open.
Let me only be free to speak
with this incredible voice.

Poems are my escape
let no person take away
what has been given
to me from God.

VERSION OF ME – II

Like no other version from the past
even did any good that was not
the best version of me.

Where city lies
lived a girl who just
needed a bit more from her life.
Another version of me was there somewhere.

She has always seen the world differently
no person could describe how
versions make their own mistakes.

Later on doubts became visions
faded past has taken
my youth has been unshaken.

Future not here quite yet
but sit and relax
enjoy this true story that
exactly happened from the beginning.

Even though versions of me was
not a proud moment
I still survived.
Now take it in while this settles inside.

www.ingramcontent.com/pod-product-compliance
Lightning Source LLC
LaVergne TN
LVHW021548080426
835509LV00019B/2915